Picking up
the pieces

Prayers for life
and all that stuff

Pete Townsend

**kevin
mayhew**

First published in Great Britain in 2002 by Kevin Mayhew Ltd
Buxhall, Stowmarket, Suffolk IP14 3BW
Tel: +44 (0) 1449 737978 Fax: +44 (0) 1449 737834
E-mail: info@kevinmayhewltd.com

www.kevinmayhew.com

9 8 7 6 5 4 3 2 1 0

ISBN 978 1 84003 852 1
Catalogue No. 1500478

Cover design by Angela Selfe
Edited and typeset by Elisabeth Bates
Printed and bound in Great Britain

Contents

Acknowledgements

Loads of thanks to Ed and Jane for the loan of their ears and to Billy and Co for the 'Hey up! 'Ow's it goin'?'

Above all I must thank my co-conspirator: God, who has gone beyond the realms of logic and reason to listen while I've off-loaded all sorts of things from my emotional swamp.

Thanks to Liz who also provides a listening ear and the occasional sane comment!

As ever, Ruth, I love you.

Introduction

Trying to find words to express the way you feel can often seem like attempting to eat soup with a chopstick ... not impossible, but likely to cause a huge amount of frustration, embarrassment and confusion. Even more annoying is trying to say how you feel to someone who already knows what you're going to say, has seen it all before, was with you when it happened and has the ability to do anything about anything!

Chatting to God can be difficult when the last thing you feel like doing is talking. What do you say? Should every other word be a thee, thou, hath or verily sort of thing? And, let's face it, should we really admit to having a few minor faults when there are so many other people with far greater faults than our own? Anyway, hasn't God got enough to do without being pestered all the time with our trivial problems?

The bottom line is that God loves us for who we are, not what we are supposed to be. Thinking that God is some far-off supreme being who is only interested in perfection is in the same league as believing that the earth is flat, politicians don't tell lies and that chocolate in no way affects our calorie intake.

The simple truth is that God enjoys nothing better than when we are honest and face up to the fact that being perfect is something we'll never be in this life. And why should we pretend that nothing's wrong when our hearts are almost at breaking point?

Trying to deal with hurt, anger, doubt, fear, loneliness, love and other assorted toffees is much more fun when you allow God to get involved in helping you to pick up the pieces.

Acceptance

A ten-letter word that means it doesn't hurt anymore . . . yeah, 'Acceptance'. It's that one word that can lift the weight of the world from our shoulders and dump it somewhere else. Without it, we feel downtrodden, weighed down, under pressure, at odds with everything and everybody.

When we feel a part of things and accepted as a part of what's going on, then we feel elated, happy with life and what it might throw at us. When, standing on the outside looking in, we sniff and tell the world, 'I don't care. If they can't accept me for who I am then that's their loss,' and then walk away with our chin scraping the floor, who are we trying to fool?

The real hassle is thinking that because we feel as if nobody is interested in us, God also doesn't care whether we breathe or suffocate in a bowl of Weetabix. Nothing could be further from the truth. I mean, how could a couple of Weetabix cause your breathing tackle to cease functioning?

Honestly though, can you really say that no matter what the situation, you don't think, even for a millisecond, that God might just be a little bit preoccupied with some other global problem? Have a read of these prayers and see what I mean.

Lord,
I suppose I don't like to think about it too much,
you know,
all those annoying ways that *other* people
behave, act, speak and just, well, you know, live.

Why can't they all be like me?
It would make things so simple.
Just imagine,
    no hassles over language,
    no arguments over how or what to eat,
    no disputes over borders or land,
    no complicated debates about nationality,
    no violent confrontations about race
    or ethnic origins.
No pointing fingers
    about the way people look, their skin tone –
    in fact, no problems whatsoever.
But, there again,
    I suppose,
    knowing the human race to be what it is,
    sooner or later
    we'd find something to argue about,
    and someone, somewhere,
    would claim to be superior to other people,
    even though
    we all bleed when we're cut,
    we all cry when we're sad,
    we all crumble to dust
    when death stakes its claim.
Lord,
    I'm just so thankful
    that, despite who we are
    or what we may claim to be,
    you love us unconditionally,
    with no cultural filters

to weed out the undesirable elements
   who you'd rather not have anything to do with.
Your love knows no boundaries,
   nor skin tones,
   or anything else for that matter.
You love us, full stop, period, without end,
   for ever and ever.
Amen to that!

Lord,
   how on earth do I stop feeling
   screwed up, washed up, tied up,
   scrunched up, fed up, messed up,
   and dried up,
   without allowing all my bodily functions
   to stop working?
Because, Lord, you've got to admit,
   I do a really good imitation of a wreck,
   without a rehearsal.
It's not that I go out of my way
   to make a complete
   donkey of myself,
   it's just that some things
   are natural!
When I'm threatened,
   and mocked,
   I must try to wise up, and remember
   that some people
   are a bit touchy at times

and that it's far better to talk to you
than listen to a load of monkeys talking bananas.
So, Lord,
I'm not saying that even sharing my thoughts with you
is going to guarantee that I won't put my foot
where it isn't wanted,
but at least I'm really glad to know
that you're always with me
and would prefer a quick yelp of help
to a long silence which ends in ouch! Amen.

Romans 15:7
Honour God by accepting each other, as Christ has accepted you.

Anger

Here we go again! For some reason the duvet's on top of the wardrobe, the jangling, rattling alarm insists on going off at the most inappropriate times, the birds have decided to flock together to perform excerpts from an opera and your throat feels as if you've been gargling with road grit.

To cap it all, someone has removed the top from the toothpaste tube and wedged it into the plug-hole, the cold tap drips worse than your nose and the toilet paper has gone in search of a cute little puppy dog. Angry? You bet.

Lord, if I think too much
    there are so many things
    which make me really, really angry.
So angry that they make my head feel
    crowded, heavy, too full to think.
I can't help looking at everything else
    through angry eyes.
I don't want to feel like this,
    as if my life is one long angry statement.
Lord, take this anger from me,
    help me to do what is right in your eyes.
Help me to look beyond the anger
    and see someone whom you love,
        even though they really get under my skin at times! Amen.

Proverbs 14:17; 17:19
Fools have quick tempers,
  and no one likes you if you can't be trusted.

The wicked and the proud love trouble
  and keep begging to be hurt.

Lord,
  come on, it's not easy you know,
  trying to ignore those things
  which get on your nerves and generally drive you mad.
How can some people be so irritating?
(Do they use some kind of anti-social deodorant?)
How can some people live with themselves?
(Have they got rhinoceros skin or what?)
How can other people put up with them?
(Or are all their mates the same?)
Can you imagine having breakfast with them?
(Weetabix, pickled onions and Marmite!)
Can you imagine having to spend time with them?
(It would be like watching stones grow.)

You can?
How do you do it?
What do you mean, 'love'?
Do you mean ignoring the irritations
  and all those really awful habits that people have?
Do you mean looking for the best in someone
  even though it could take some time?

You mean it, don't you,
    that idea about love?
Being kind and watching out for each other
    sounds OK, but I'll need some help.
How are you fixed? Amen.

Christian life

Isn't life difficult enough? You know, all this breathing, washing, eating, moving about, smiling and frowning with other assorted functions and then, on top of it all, some bright amoeba suggesting that there's more to living!

If, like me, you feel that it's all just a bit confusing and that to fit everything into a week combines all the skills of a juggler, a diplomat, a politician, a brick wall and a figure-skating gorilla wearing a tutu, then perhaps some of these prayers might raise a smile, grimace, a knowing nod or a frown.

Lord, be fair –
   it isn't easy you know,
   and it's really difficult
   with a hot sausage roll in your mouth!
I can't help it,
   it's just . . . well, you know,
   not easy.
It's not that I don't care
   or that I can't be bothered;
   that's just not true,
   even though it may seem like it.
I want to chat about you
   and what you mean to me,
   but it's just not very easy.
And it's really difficult

when the jokes get out of hand;
and it's really difficult
when I can't take my eyes
off the spot on her chin.
But I'm not giving up,
I'll give it a go.
But promise me one thing –
you'll back up everything I say! Amen.

God,
a lot of the time,
I just can't get a handle on you.
I can't find answers to the questions
that rumble around my head
making everything appear unclear,
difficult to see, hard to understand.
If only I could speak to you
face to face;
ask some of those questions
that are burning my tongue;
see what it is you want me to see;
put things into perspective
so that my image of you
isn't quite so distorted.
I don't want to feel afraid
that my honesty
causes you, and other people,
a problem.

I think that
    if my questions cause them a problem,
    that's not my problem but theirs.
I'm waiting, listening.
Please tell me what you think
    and that way
    at least we're talking
    which, if what I hear is right,
    is what you wanted
    in the first place! Amen.

Lord, it feels, at times,
    that I'm walking through treacle.
Each step takes so much effort,
    and I know that the next time I put my foot down
    it's going to be messy . . . again.
I want to follow you,
    but when the going gets tough
    my feet get stuck.
It wouldn't be so much of a problem
    if everything was OK here, right now.
But, well, it's sort of sticky, you know how it is.
What with this and that, that and this,
    and plenty of bother.
I think I need you, Lord,
    to help me out.
Providing you've got
    a bucket of hot soapy water,
    scrubbing brush and a towel. Amen.

Lord,
    although I've no real idea
    how to understand the concept
    of you having three parts,
    I can relate to the idea
    that you know what it's like
    to have someone who
    acts as a parent,
    telling us what to do,
    when to do it,
    how to do it,
    and that it's for our own good
    (although we really don't want to do it,
    but who said anything about choice?),
    and you know something about being a parent,
    wondering if their child
    is going to be all right.
Are they doing as they have been told?
Who are they hanging around with?
And should they really be seen
    with those less than desirable people,
    who everybody says
    are sure to be trouble with a capital 'T'?
And you know all about that Holy Spirit bit,
    the part that most people,
    would rather leave in the margins
    of their memories,
    where it's convenient to forget
    and only drag out the details
    on special occasions,

like weddings, funerals
and getting Easter eggs.
Isn't this Holy Spirit thing
supposed to be just as important?
You know, it's the bit
that Jesus said would be with us
all the time,
even when we feel useless,
powerless and everything-less?
Lord,
help me to appreciate
all that you are,
everything that you can be
to me,
and every person
on this large lump of earth. Amen.

Matthew 22:37-39
Jesus answered:
Love the Lord your God with all your heart, soul and mind. This is the
first and most important commandment. The second most important
commandment is like this one. And it is, 'Love others as much as you
love yourself.'

Lord,
if you ask me,
this *sacrifice* thing is a bit much.
What's the point?

How can giving something away
   mean so much?
Can you tell me
   how my actions
   can change the way other people
   behave, or think or believe?
I'm not so sure
   that the best thing to do
   isn't to keep everything I've got
   and to look after myself,
   just so that other people can see
   how good you are to me.
And, just think,
   you could give me even more good things,
   just to make the point, OK?
But there is one thing that niggles me.
Somewhere along the way,
   didn't you do something for me
   that changed everything,
   and made it possible to get to know
   God the Father, like a friend, a dad,
   someone you like to have around?
And, when I think about it a little more,
   didn't Jesus make all this a reality
   by giving up everything he had,
   everything he could be,
   everything everybody wanted him to be,
   just so that me and you could get to know each other?
I'm not saying I understand this *sacrifice* thing,
   but however it works,

it's made a difference to me,
and I suppose that's the point of it all.
Lord, help me to make a difference
to those people around me.
And, just a final thing,
do you know anybody
who might like
half a packet of custard cream biscuits? Amen.

Lord,
I can't always say exactly when I may need your help,
or precisely *where* I'll need it,
but I think I'll always know *why*
I need your help,
your love,
your understanding,
and the occasional bit of patience
for those times when nothing I say or do seems right.
Why I need you around is simply because,
no matter how hard I try not to
screw everything up with such finesse,
whatever I try to do
always ends up with my own,
totally unique,
absolutely unmistakable,
foot in mouth,
finger in the eye,
tread on foot trademark
that everyone knows

is my way of doing things,
that nobody else would have thought of
(or wouldn't even dream of doing if they had any sense).
What I'm saying, Lord,
is that even when I do my best,
it isn't always the best that everyone expects.
So, could we come to some sort of arrangement,
where you get involved in my everyday life,
every single day of my existence,
to make sure
that we all get used to having
a touch of the extraordinary
in our ordinary lives? Amen.

John 14:23-24
Jesus replied:
If anyone loves me they will obey me. Then my Father will love them, and we will come to them and live in them. But anyone who doesn't love me, won't obey me. What they have heard me say doesn't really come from me, but from the Father who sent me.

Lord, thank you for 'OUCH'!
Without it I wouldn't know what to say.
Like the 'ouch' when I stub my toe,
or the 'ouch' when I try to move a solid object with my head!
Especially the 'ouch'
when someone stabs my ego
with a well-aimed word.

I think 'ouch' is such a useful word.
It has the ring of pain
   where other words have no echo.
I understand 'ouch' when it registers in my brain,
   like it affects the parts
   that other words can't reach.
I can feel the 'ouch'
   even though I'm not hungry,
   as I watch the skeletal forms
   crying in their stillness on the TV screen.
I can feel the 'ouch'
   even though I'm not grieving,
   as I read about the fingers of death
   pointing at the innocent.
I can feel the 'ouch'
   even though I'm not in the line of fire,
   as I listen to the powerless voices
   of refugees walking to misery
   I don't always understand,
   I can't say I know why.
But you've been there before me,
   you know the misery.
You gave us the choice to anaesthetise pain,
   to ignore the hurting and point the finger of blame.
Without the 'ouch'
   I might not recognise pain,
   and then it would be too late
   when pain recognises me. Amen.

Church

While Clerics consider, Theologians theorise, Deacons deliberate and Academics argue, everybody else wonders what on earth the 'Church' is all about!

What can any of us answer? The nearest I can offer is that it's something that takes years of building; it should always be the centre of a community; it's often laughed at but very rarely gets the joke; sometimes, and only sometimes, it earns a little respect yet is in need of constant attention and repair . . . and I'm not talking about the woodwork, bricks and stained glass!

The 'Church' should always be identified as the group of people who share their faith together and with the community. It operates at its best when it can see the funny side of life and earns respect for the way it's willing to get its hands dirty and its knees scraped. The 'Church' should always be willing to go out of its way to look after each other and the needs of the community. There should never be a time when it can take a back-seat, smile smugly and watch the world go by.

Seeing the Church for what it is may take some time, but it's worth the effort.

Lord,
    I really can't get my head around
    all this 'thee, thou and therefore' stuff.
It drives me round the bend and over the hill.
What does it all mean?

Is it some sort of code for the initiated?
A kind of secret language
    that only those in the know understand?
Do we need a translator or interpreter
    to explain what's going on
    and what we need to do?
Should there be a sort of 'idiots' guide'
    to help us say the 'right' things at the 'right' time? –
    so that we don't stand up when we should be sitting down.
Perhaps you could suggest
    that someone puts a few dictionaries
    next to the hymn books,
    although I really think
    that we'd never sing a word or a note.
We'd be too busy looking in the dictionary
    trying to find out
    what we were singing about,
    or what we were trying to say
    if only we knew what we'd said!
I think we need
    the Holy Spirit
    to descend on a few of the congregation
    and get them to speak
    in a language
    that we can all understand.
Until that time,
    you'll have to guess what I mean
    'cos the only word I've got sorted
    comes at the end of a line. Amen.

1 Corinthians 12:12-31

The body of Christ has many different parts, just as any other body does. Some of us are Jews, and others are Gentiles. Some of us are slaves, and others are free. But God's Spirit baptised each of us and made us part of the body of Christ. Now we each drink from that same Spirit.

Our bodies don't have just one part. They are many parts. Suppose a foot says, 'I'm not a hand, and so I'm not part of the body.' Wouldn't the foot still belong to the body?

Or suppose an ear says, 'I'm not an eye, and so I'm not part of the body.' Wouldn't the ear still belong to the body? If our bodies were only an eye, we couldn't hear a thing. And if they were only an ear, we couldn't smell a thing. But God has put all parts of our body together in the way he decided is best.

A body isn't really a body, unless there is more than one part. It takes many parts to make a single body. That's why the eyes cannot say they don't need the hands. That's also why the head cannot say it doesn't need the feet. In fact, we cannot get along without the parts of the body that seem to be the weakest. We take special care to dress up some parts of our bodies. We are modest about our personal parts, but we don't have to be modest about other parts.

God put our bodies together in such a way that even the parts that seem the least important are valuable. He did this to make all parts of the body work together smoothly, with each part caring about the others. If one part of our body hurts, we hurt all over. If one part of our body is honoured, the whole body will be happy.

Together you are the body of Christ. Each one of you is part of his body. First, God chose some people to be apostles and prophets and teachers for the church. But he also chose some to perform miracles or heal the sick or help others or be leaders or speak different kinds of languages. Not everyone is an apostle. Not everyone is a prophet. Not everyone is a teacher. Not everyone can perform miracles. Not everyone can heal the sick. Not everyone can speak different kinds of languages. Not everyone can tell what these languages mean. I want you to desire the best gifts. So I will show you a much better way.

Lord,
    this church thing,
    is at best a bit odd,
    and at worst,
    the most boring time I've ever had to spend
    (apart from sitting through a documentary on painting ceilings).
But the funny thing is, Lord,
    that when you look around
    at all these bodies
    gathered in one place
    to chat about you,
    sing a bit,
    and listen to the vicar
    try and tell a joke
    without giving away the punchline,
    or forget he was telling a joke
    in the first place.
Then,
    when we're having a cup of tea,
    and a biscuit if some little grubby fingers haven't nicked them all,
    there seems to be an odd assortment of people
    who, for one reason or another,
    want to know more about you.

And, Lord,
    I'm really glad
    that you love
    every size, shape, colour, texture and hue,
    and you don't care one little bit
    about status, prestige, earnings, cars,
    gadgets or designer clothes,
    because you care about the person,
    the body inside
    which is vulnerable, sensitive and needs
    a lot of TLC.
So, thanks,
    thanks that you love me, and him, and her
    and every single fragile human being,
    wherever and whatever. Amen.

Confusion

Confusion: the art of taking two + two and getting $E=MC^2$. Life can often seem like a supermarket; we enter with a detailed list of what we know we want and need, and then get distracted by the range of choice and special offers. Even though the 'buy one get one free' and 'buy two get the third half price' appear to be bargains, we know that ultimately, at the check-out, we have to pay for everything that we've chosen.

Admittedly, there are those people who refuse to be seduced by the bargain offers and stick to the list. But even then they are faced with a bewildering array of options with 25 per cent less this and no added that, not counting the additive free, calorific value and packaging! When faced with so much choice there are very rarely any easy options or answers. So, what do we do? Don't ask me, I'm as confused as you are!

Proverbs 20:24
How can we know what will happen to us when the Lord alone decides?

OK, Lord
    so what's going on?
Why do I feel this way?
It can't be all my fault, can it?
Well, see it my way:

if I spend all my time
  wondering what other people think or feel,
  how will I ever get
  to where I want to go?
How will I ever get what I want?
Although I have to admit
  that at times I feel like I'm chewing sand,
  or walking through treacle.
Perhaps I shouldn't struggle
  and keep yelling in your ear.
Perhaps I should listen,
  take the time to see and hear
  just how much you love me,
  and him and her. Amen.

Lord,
  getting confused
  seems to be an occupational hazard
  of living.
Everyone has an opinion
  and everyone insists they're right!
Words seem to surround me
  like a dust cloud on a hot day.
They blur my vision and dull my senses.
I'm not sure which way to turn.
Do this, do that,
  don't do this, don't do that.
What am I supposed to do?
I need to be able

to pick out the truth
from a pile of garbage.
I need to see the truth
stand out like a neon light
on a dark night.
Help me, Lord,
to know you,
to see, hear and know the truth
in a land of confusion. Amen.

Father,
I'm sorry if I seem to have a bag over my head at times!
It's not that I don't notice things,
I just don't always see them!
You know how it is;
so much to do and so little time to do it.
Or maybe I don't have a lot of time
for those things which seem hard.
I don't use excuses;
I really do like to watch an obscure documentary on TV!
You can always learn something,
and it's better than seeing what you don't want to see.
If I look too hard,
I might see something which needs to be done,
like talking to someone I don't really know.
It's nice, me and you,
two's company and three's a crowd.
But I seem to remember
that Jesus liked talking to crowds! Amen.

Death

We usually enter this world in a horizontal position and exit it in the same posture, so why make the bit in-between difficult by standing up?

Hang on a minute! Wouldn't we miss out on a few things in life if we never raised our head from the pillow? When you come to think of it, there's so much to see and do on our journey through the organic patchwork quilt that maintaining a horizontal position seems like a waste of precious time.

It's a bit like a lost property office really. (Life! What did you think I was on about?) The office is a collection of the unusual and the mundane, the weird and the wonderful, the wacky and the obvious and within it all something to discover and experience whatever the outcome of our rummage through the contents of a moth-eaten suitcase; it's all something to celebrate.

And that, possibly, is how we should view death, a reminder to appreciate life.

Lord,
    it's a good thing
    that we have no idea,
    know absolutely zilch,
    haven't the faintest hope
    of being able to predict
    when we will finally wave goodbye
    to the human race.
But as I take each breath
    (which better not be my last!)

I want to say
thanks for my life to date,
and as each day passes
may there be many, many more of them.
Although life may have
its ups and downs,
I would prefer
more of the ups and less of the downs.
And that goes for those people
who may be inclined to think
that their life is going downhill big time.
Give me the courage, Lord,
to make a difference,
to give a helping hand
whenever it's needed,
even at those times
when it feels as if
I'm sitting in a pit
waiting for a rain cloud
to take its juice somewhere else.
Help me, help us,
to be the difference
between a smile and a frown. Amen.

Psalm 23:4
I may walk through valleys as dark as death,
but I won't be afraid.
You are with me,
and your shepherd's rod makes me feel safe.

Decisions

Decisions, decisions, decisions, decisions, decisions, decisions and even more decisions. Our days seem to revolve constantly around deciding when, and if, we're going to emerge from under the duvet or at precisely what time we want to crawl under the warming folds of the sleep sandwich. You could say, why let the bed get cold in the first place by leaving it just when you'd found the most comfortable spot? But still, that's another decision to make. Oh hum, decisions are never easy but the need to decide seems to come along with alarming monotony.

Lord, I may not have much to offer,
    I'm not always sure what I have to give.
There are times when all I can think about is me,
    what I want and what would make me feel good.
Lord, it isn't always easy to think what other people need,
    especially when there are so many things I want.
But you have promised to watch out for me,
    I'm never out of your sight or out of your thinking.
You want the best for me and you gave your best for me,
    nothing I can give can match that!
Thank you for your gift of life,
    the greatest gift of all. Amen.

Romans 12:1-2
Dear friends, God is good. So I beg you to offer your bodies to him as a living sacrifice, pure and pleasing. That's the most sensible way to

serve God. Don't be like the people of the world, but let God change the way you think. Then you will know how to do everything that is good and pleasing to him.

Lord,
    now, I'm really lost here,
    I've no idea which way to go,
    what to do
    or whether to do anything at all.
If I turn left
    I'll upset those on the right,
    and if I turn right
    I'll upset those on the left.
If I move forward
    people will think
    I'm trying to leave them behind
    and if I move back
    people will think
    I'm being evasive.
I try to do the right thing, honest,
    but trying to please
    so many people
    with so many points of view,
    opinions,
    ideas
    (and the occasional plague of stubborn behaviour),
    I'll end up doing the wrong thing
    at the wrong time
    for the wrong people.

I think it's about time
  to get a bit of advice.
The confusion is killing me
  (or I'll be killing someone if this goes on much longer).
So, as the Creator and all that,
  I reckon you might have a few good ideas.
Do you mind sharing some? Amen.

Doubt

Tense, nervous headache? Feeling a little uncertain of things? Has a certain vagueness crept into your thinking? Well, welcome to the human race!

If anyone ever tells you that they never doubted so and so, or such and such for one moment, then the only sure thing is that you've been listening to someone who's protesting their innocence a bit too much!

Doubt, it's a fact of life. At times doubt can be extremely healthy, particularly when you question your chances of wading through an alligator infested swamp on a pair of wooden stilts...and still be able to count ten toes at the other side.

Although it's usually considered to be a negative thing, doubt is just a moment in time when your head decides to take time out before it goes into meltdown. The best bit about doubt is having friends around who've been there, got the T-shirt and still don't tell you what to do!

Matthew 21:21
But Jesus said to them, 'If you have faith and don't doubt, I promise that you can do what I did to this tree. And you will be able to do even more. You can tell this mountain to get up and jump into the sea, and it will.'

Lord,
    at times there seem so many voices,
    so many people

shouting, calling, pointing,
I can't hear myself think.
What am I expected to do?
Whose voice should I listen to?
Where can I look?

Then, in the middle of the noise,
the confusion, the chaos,
I think I can just hear
a small, persistent voice
whispering, calling, comforting.
It's a voice I recognise,
a voice that I've come to appreciate;
always there, always speaking
with a love that's awesome;
a love that's there for me.
Everything else becomes distant,
as I turn my ear towards the voice,
and hear you speak my name.
You're here for me, I'm listening. Amen.

Lord, I don't understand philosophy,
I can't get my head around psychology,
and theology leaves me cold.
I'm not trying to make trouble,
or cause anyone a problem.
I just want to be honest,
well, as honest as I can be.

Don't get me wrong,
    I'm not saying I know it all,
    I'm glad I don't,
    know it all, I mean.
I want my faith to be real,
    not based on some second-hand account,
    or a set of rules which make me choke.
If I'm going to believe in you,
    properly, not some Sunday saint,
    or weekday wonder,
    but real, like a proper relationship
    between two hearts,
    then help me see the truth
    of who you are,
    and what you mean to me. Amen.

Lord,
    life feels like a game of skittles –
    you've guessed it! I'm not the ball.
Even when I try to keep my eyes open
    to avoid taking a knock.
Bang! Out of nowhere the ball comes flying,
    and I'm left staring at the sky.
Sometimes things seem to be going wrong all the time.
Is it really me or something I said?
I try so hard to do the right thing,
    but I don't think that other people think the way I do.
Or do some people enjoy knocking me down?
It certainly seems that way.

You must know the feeling:
  'can't do right for doing wrong'.
Sometimes I think that my face doesn't fit,
  and it hurts like hell,
  trying to squeeze into a mould
  that's just not my shape.

Still, it's a good thing
  that you don't turn your back
  or pretend to be deaf
  when my mouth opens and the verbal begins.
Lord, thank you
  that no matter what,
  you are for me,
  and you want the best for me.
Thanks for being there, or rather, here. Amen.

Faith

Faith, as JC said, is like a mustard seed . . . a little goes a long way and gets things moving! The only problem is that you can get mustard seeds from supermarkets or health shops ready to use, but faith seems to require an awful lot of nurturing!

Anyway, I'm not particularly sure I want to rearrange mountain ranges, or relocate the Himalayas close to Timbuktu. But I wouldn't mind feeling that I wasn't stuck in the middle of an ocean in a leaking boat, no paddle and only a parrot to keep me company!

If faith is knowing that you're never alone, whatever the situation you find yourself up to your neck in, then can I have some please?

Lord, if I think too much
    there are so many things
    which make me really, really angry.
So angry that they make my head feel
    crowded, heavy, too full to think.
I can't help looking at everything else
    through angry eyes.
I don't want to feel like this,
    as if my life is one long angry statement.
Lord, take this anger from me,
    help me to do what is right in your eyes.
Help me to look beyond the anger
    and see someone whom you love,
        even though they can really get under my skin at times! Amen.

Lord,
    I'm really finding life
    kind of frustrating.
So many things
    demanding my attention,
    wanting my time,
    eating away at my sanity
    until I can't remember
    what it was I was supposed to be doing
    in the first place.
Sometimes I walk into a room
    and then spend the next ten minutes
    wondering what I'm doing there!
I look around for a sign,
    a clue to my action.
Why, when, how, what for?
And Lord,
    if I'm honest
    that's exactly how I feel
    when I go to church.
It's not that I don't want to be there
    but it would be nice
    if I had a clue
    as to what I was supposed to be doing there!
It's a good job that my faith
    isn't in tradition, buildings or committees,
    or even how many times
    someone remembers my name,
    but my faith is in the One
    who gave his all for me. Amen.

Jesus, at times it's really difficult,
    really difficult to understand what you mean.
It's even more difficult to do what you say,
    even when we understand.
It's not easy.
I know it's about faith, it's about trust.
Easy to say, but not easy to put into practice.
As I lift my eyes
    allow me to see what you meant
    by dying to live;
    by giving to receive.
Thank you for my choice.
Help me to use my choice,
    rather than ignore it.
You died for me to live.
What more can I say? Amen.

Lord,
    at times I would rather chew sand
    than do what you want.
I'm not being a pain,
    just trying to find my way about.
The trouble is,
    although I'm not trying to be a pain,
    I'm in pain
    because I have a tendency to walk into things,
    to trip over the obvious,
    to attempt a backward somersault
    with a bag over my head.

I think I'm learning
   that your love for me
   is so great
   that following your ways
   makes a lot of sense. Amen.

Psalm 27
You, Lord, are the light that keeps me safe.
I am not afraid of anyone.
You protect me, and I have no fears.
Brutal people may attack and try to kill me,
   but they will stumble.
Fierce enemies may attack, but they will fall.
Armies may surround me, but I won't be afraid;
   war may break out, but I will trust you.

I ask only one thing, Lord:
   let me live in your house every day of my life
   to see how wonderful you are
   and to pray in your temple.

In times of trouble, you will protect me.
You will hide me in your tent
   and keep me safe on top of a mighty rock.
You will let me defeat all of my enemies.
Then I will celebrate, as I enter your tent
   with animal sacrifices and songs of praise.

Please listen when I pray!
Have pity. Answer my prayer.

My heart tells me to pray.
I am eager to see your face,
  so don't hide from me.
I am your servant, and you have helped me.
Don't turn from me in anger.
You alone keep me safe. Don't reject or desert me.
Even if my father and mother should desert me,
  you will take care of me.
Teach me to follow, Lord,
  and lead me on the right path
  because of my enemies.
Don't let them do to me what they want.
People tell lies about me and make terrible threats,
  but I know I will live to see how kind you are.
Trust the Lord! Be brave and strong and trust the Lord.

Lord,
    I've heard that
    Jesus said if you had faith
    the size of a mustard seed
    then you could do amazing things.
Well, Lord,
    I'm not sure
    how big a mustard seed is exactly,
    but I think that my sort of faith
    doesn't compare with that of the seed.
My faith is, well, sort of,
    precisely, or thereabouts,

about as big
as a speck of dust
or even smaller.
It might be better
to look at my faith through a microscope,
and then, just possibly,
you might see a tiny,
or even smaller,
speck in the distance.
I'm not quite proud of this fact, Lord,
I'm even a bit embarrassed really.
But at least I'm not going to shout my mouth off
about something I know very little about.
So, I think we've got a bit of work to do,
you know, me and you, Lord,
because there's not a lot I can do
to change the situation,
but I've heard that you can do
sort of amazing things,
out of nothing, nowhere,
in the blink of an eye, sort of.
And I was wondering,
if we can get together on this one,
and maybe, just maybe,
I might be able to see a difference
in the way I trust you.
And that really would be a miracle. Amen.

Lord,
    I've got my eyes wide shut.
If I keep them open
    I can see so many other needs
    that get in the way of mine.
I've so much on my mind
    but you keep interrupting!
Can I get a word in edgeways
    to inform you about some of the things
    that need your attention?
It's all right reminding me about other people
    and their needs,
    but have you seen my list?
If I spend much more of my time
    thinking of others
    most of my prayers will have passed
    their sell-by date!
Either that,
    or by the time I get around to asking you
    about some of my needs
    I've fallen asleep.
So Lord,
    let's make a deal.
    I'll pray for me,
    if you'll look after other people.
Or should it be,
    I'll pray for other people,
    while you look after me? Amen.

Fear

'Who's afraid of the big bad turnip? er, potato? erm, manglewurzle? I know, spider! No? All right then, what are you afraid of? You don't have to answer that if even saying the words aloud makes your ears sweat and your knees go a funny colour.

Different things seem to frighten different people. What may seem a positive, or even exciting experience to one person, getting married for instance, might turn someone else into a jibbering wreck. (Or is that what happens after you get married? You tell me.)

You might laugh at danger or shrug your shoulders with indifference at the sight of a bowl full of prunes (scares the living daylights out of me!). But, given the right circumstances, you just might stand back in amazement at my ability to face cold tapioca pudding without flinching, although I might not feel the same on a dark and stormy night with the wind howling and the rain beating against the window . . . scary.

Lord,
    although the desert sands may freeze,
    and the oceans dry up,
    your love remains.
Although the mountains may crumble,
    and the sky turn black,
    your love remains.
My Lord, you are King.

Even though I see death and destruction
    and rivers of tears,

my Lord, you are King.
Even though I see hatred and violence
and broken hearts,
my Lord, you are King.

Let me remember you
when the clouds gather
and the rain falls.
Let me remember you
when the thunder sounds
and my feet tremble.
My Lord, you are King.

You keep me secure
in your warm embrace.
Your love is as high as the heavens
and as deep as the oceans.
My Lord, you are King. Amen.

Hebrews 13:5-6
Don't fall in love with money. Be satisfied with what you have. The Lord has promised that he will not leave or desert us. That should make you feel like saying,
'The Lord helps me!
Why should I be afraid
of what people can do to me?'

Lord,
   I realise it sounds daft,
   possibly really stupid
   in the warm light of the day,
   but I just can't help
   looking behind me
   whenever I walk upstairs to bed.
Now, please don't laugh,
   I know it's irrational,
   that there's nothing there,
   but you never know,
   one day there just might be
   something which will throw my life
   into confusion, disarray,
   and make it seem like
   the sun's gone to sleep.

You see,
   the stairs
   are my life.
It's my journey
   from birth to the future.
And I really need to know
   that you're there,
   right behind me,
   beside me, in front of me,
   watching my feet
   so that I don't trip over my own shadow. Amen.

Lord,
   you are the light of my life.
But sometimes,
   just sometimes,
   it seems very dark.
Dark enough to make me feel cold,
   lonely,
   isolated from the warmth of your love.
It feels as if the long fingers of fear
   creep around me, over me, swallowing the light.
I want to run,
   hide, cover my face with my hands.
But they just make it seem even darker.
Lord, remind me
   that you are my strong tower
   where I can run to.
And, Lord,
   remind me that putting my hands in front of my face
   only makes things worse,
   like trusting my own senses
   to get me through the darkness.
Lord, light my life,
   light my way as I walk each day with you. Amen.

Psalm 56:10-11
I praise your promises!
I trust you and I am not afraid. No one can harm me.

Forgiveness

To forgive someone is frightening. It can leave you vulnerable and open to criticism from anyone. However, before you decide to play safe and hold a grudge against the world and the snooker club, take a look at the word 'forgive'.

Take the first three letters: 'FOR'. To be 'for' someone is to be positive towards them, to encourage them and have their best interests at heart. The other four letters, 'GIVE', are again a positive action. To 'give' is to offer something that you feel would make a difference to that person's life.

In a nutshell, 'forgiveness' is an action, a positive statement, something which can make a difference. Go on, live dangerously.

Psalm 32:5
So I confessed my sins and told them all to you.
I said, 'I'll tell the Lord each one of my sins.'
Then you forgave me and took away my guilt.

Lord,
    you know I used to be so sure
    that it wasn't ever my fault,
    but now I'm not so sure.
Things seem so complicated,
    so confusing
    that I feel as if I'm on a roundabout,

can't remember where it started
and don't know if it's ever going to end.
I know this can't continue,
    life is being wasted
    going around in circles
    getting dizzy.
Help me, Lord,
    to forgive
    and be forgiven.
Help me,
    be with me
    especially when I screw up with such finesse. Amen.

Gossip

Can you imagine what journalists would do without the odd bit of scandal or innuendo? And, it goes without saying, it doesn't really matter whether the 'facts' are remotely accurate, does it? We can't have grains of truth spoiling the fun, can we? Besides, a good bit of gossip keeps us entertained.

Have you ever considered why we seem to delight in reading about the peculiar habits of soap stars, or how much a Hollywood superstar pays to have a personal chef to cater for their pet earwig? Is it really necessary for us to know the contents of a pop star's dustbin? Or why a television newsreader wears pyjama bottoms when informing the public about the latest government exposé?

Why do we find the slush and mush on other people so fascinating? Could it be that we lead such boring lives that any bit of gossip, or even something ever so slightly off-white, grabs our attention like a magnet does iron filings? Might it even be that we take great pleasure in seeing someone suffer as a result of a malicious word? Are we that jealous of someone's success that we throw a party when we read such delightful headlines as:

'Shocking discovery in small room! A Mrs Gladys Pipsqueak, a highly reputable cleaning lady, is currently under sedation after finding a piece of navel fluff lurking on the bathroom floor of one of her clients . . .'

With such glorious details is it worth checking the facts first? Anyway, listen, have you heard about that bloke at No. 23, and her from the deli counter . . .?

Dear Lord, do you know the latest?
I heard it from a reliable source,
    I got it from a friend who lives next door to someone,
    whose second cousin saw a friend in the supermarket.
I'm not one to gossip, I speak as I find!
I don't cause trouble, I just say what's on my mind.
You know what they say, 'a trouble shared is a trouble halved'!
I'm doing a favour,
    just spreading the load.
It's no skin off my nose,
    I'm happy to help.
So, if you feel a bit busy and need someone to tell,
    don't hesitate to call me, I'm always in.
I mean, how can I feel sorry for someone,
    if I don't know what's what?
I don't want the gory detail,
    just the juicy bits will do!
Now, what was I going to tell you?
I bet you know already.
Still, good news will keep,
    until the next time I hear a scandal
    which needs a little 'help'! Amen.

Proverbs 11:11-13
When God blesses his people, their city prospers,
    but deceitful liars can destroy a city.
It's stupid to say bad things about your neighbours.
If your are sensible, you will keep quiet.
A gossip tells everything,
    but a true friend will keep a secret.

Hassle

'If only . . . if it wasn't for . . . I'm up to my armpits in . . . wouldn't life be easier if . . . ?'

It's got to be said, but life just ain't life without hiccups!

Fortunately, most hassle is just a temporary lump in the mattress of life. The problem is that at the time the 'lump' seems to find our most sensitive spots and aggravates us with a seemingly never-ending attack on the flesh!

How are we supposed to deal with these types of aggravations and irritations, and still keep our sense of balance?

The universal answer may be to have a good old moan and groan, to let everybody know just how big an aggravating lump we are putting up with (and no, Mrs, I don't mean your partner!) and put up with the inconvenience as well as any martyr you care to name.

I suppose there has to be some bright spark out there who would suggest that learning to live with, and deal with, these hassles is the only way to learn how to cope when things really get gritty. Oh well, whatever. All I can say is that hassles are like having a stone in your shoe: before long you have to stop and do something about it, but you know it's not going to be too long before there's another stone intent on putting a hole in your sock!

Lord,
    trouble seems to have a habit of getting under my skin.
It itches and aggravates,
        and the more I scratch it, the more it itches.

How does trouble find me?
I certainly don't go looking for it,
     it seems to find me wherever I am.
It's not always my fault,
     well, sometimes maybe, but not every time!
Please help me to see things your way,
     because my way sometimes misses the point
     or makes the trouble worse!
I need to see things your way,
     because I have the knack
     of sometimes missing the obvious
     or making up my mind
     without knowing all the facts.
You seemed to know what you were doing
     on the way into Jerusalem.
Even though others thought it odd
     that a king should ride a donkey.
But you had other thoughts in mind,
     beyond what could be imagined
     by your closest friends.
Prince of Peace, take my troubles
     and bring your peace instead. Amen.

Lord,
     well, it's kind of difficult.
I suppose with all your omniscience
     you know what's going on or what's supposed to be happening
     but it isn't turning out according to plan.
I thought everything was fine

until everything fell apart
   like the proverbial pack of cards.
And now here I am, wanting to know
   what on earth you were doing
   which took your mind off my situation?
Am I so inconsequential?
Or were things wrong from the beginning?
I really did think that I knew what I was doing
   even though I hadn't got a clue
   what was going on, down and along
   until I started to go under.
So, here I am.
Better late than never I always say.
I would have chatted sooner
   but I was so busy doing this, that and the other,
   and thought you might be a touch busy
   dealing with all those things
   that occupy the creator of all things.
And now, having realised
   that I've put my foot in it big time,
   I thought I'd better get around to asking
   how we're going to sort this mess out.
I know it might seem a cheek
   to ask for your help after the event,
   but, as I said earlier, better late than never.
I can't promise I'll do things any different
   the next time,
   but it's good to know that you're a very forgiving sort,
   which is just as well because,
   although I don't mean to,

I somehow always forget
to check things out with you first,
but still, I get around to it, eventually.
And as I always say,
better late than never. Amen.

Lord,
you know I've been having a few problems lately.
But there's nothing to worry about,
I'm only up to my ankles
in the emotional swamp.
I could mention others
who are not so lucky.
I only hope
that you've taught them how to swim.
If I'm honest,
things have been tough for a while.
You know how it is,
one thing leads to another and . . .
whoops, it's up to my waist.
There's still nothing to worry about.
I've dealt with this before.
Not too successfully though,
as you know.
Oh, I seem to have sunk up to my armpits.
Look, this isn't funny.
I'm really trying, you know,
to keep up appearances
but it doesn't seem to help.

In fact, it makes matters worse,
    because everyone thinks I'm all right,
    and I'm not.
So, if you've got a moment,
    could you lift me out?
And it would help a lot
    if there was someone else about. Amen.

Psalm 42:5
Why am I discouraged? Why am I restless?
I trust you! And I will praise you again
  because you help me, and you are my God.

Lord,
    I've gone through every emotion in the dictionary.
I've shouted until my throat hurts.
My head aches with the thoughts
    of senseless violence,
    of mindless actions
    that have robbed people
    of their hopes, their dreams, their lives.
I can't pretend to understand
    or find an answer
    to the jigsaw of events
    that froze a moment in time
    for ever.
Tears sometimes say more
    than mere words can express.

A cry from the heart
    speaks more wisdom
    than a thousand wise men.
But all I can say is
    I don't understand, Lord.
    All I can pray is that somehow,
    for all those involved,
    you would bring peace
    and understanding,
    while I place my life
    in your hands.
Keep me safe, keep me willing
    to hear your voice and your heart. Amen.

Lord,
    you may understand –
    but I certainly don't –
    why things happen to me
    the way they do.
At times I feel like a magnet
    that attracts problems looking for a home.
Sometimes
    I go to sleep feeling on top of the world
    and wake up the next morning
    with a head
    that feels as if it's just been trampled on
    by a herd of cattle.
Also, you may have noticed,
    I've developed a bit of a stoop when I walk.

Having the weight of the world
   on one's shoulders
    is a bit much for anyone to bear.
I've been let down, put down,
   ignored and rejected.
But rather
   than place my trust
   in anyone
   or any system
   that will only make me feel
   more screwed up than I am already,
   I'm turning to you,
   with all my baggage
   and dodgy ways –
   because you don't seem to care
   that I'm not a neat, sorted, top-notch
   kind of person –
   you love me just the way I am. Amen.

Sometimes, God,
   I want to scream and shout . . .
   at YOU.
It's like I've been walking for so long,
   my feet ache, I'm hungry,
   and I'm desperate for something to drink.
I feel like just falling down
   flat, horizontal,
   and not getting up again,
   at least not for a while.

Do you understand what I'm trying to say?
I'm tired, God.
All this,
   everything,
   everybody,
   just seem far too much to cope with.
At times I feel as if I've got a problem
   for every letter of the alphabet,
   and some more!
When times are tough,
   when I'm hurting,
   crying with frustration,
   angry at the world and everybody in it,
   it would be really neat
   to be able to snap my fingers
   and say: 'Job done!'
But you know, and I know,
   that if that was all there was to it,
   I'd probably find myself in the same mess,
   the same hassle,
   feeling the same hurt, frustration and anger,
   as I did the time before,
   and the time before that, and the time before that,
   etc., etc., etc., for ever, amen.
Whenever I feel like this, God,
   just give me a hug,
   a smile and a nudge,
   and tell me that I'm not on my own.
That together we're a team,
   me and you. Amen.

Loneliness

How can anyone say they're lonely when there are approximately 6,500 million people treading on the same planet? Yet, despite the overwhelming odour of 13,000 million feet, we can feel totally, absolutely and completely isolated, on our own, with no one around who can understand how we feel!

All too often, feeling like a calorie addict at a weight-watchers' convention, we recognise only one thing . . . loneliness. We can be in a room full of friends, family and other assorted wrinkles; we can be standing in the middle of a bus queue with other people who also think that the Number 52 bus has become yet another victim of the Bermuda Triangle; we can be sitting in a cinema full of popcorn crunchers, or exchanging germs with other cough- and mucus-infested people at the doctor's surgery – whatever it is, we can still look around and think that we have nothing in common with anybody, that nobody understands the way we feel and that everyone else is sorted and at one with the world.

However we look at it, feeling lonely hurts. And, if you've never tried it before, it doesn't hurt as much to have a rant at someone who really does know how you feel . . . and why.

Lord,
    being without friends
    is like being alone in a desert
    with only the sand and wind to keep me company.

Lord,
    being without friends
    is like a song
    without a voice to sing.

Lord,
    being without friends
    is like a book
    which has no words.

Help me to be your voice
    to those who need to hear
    a whisper of hope,
    a whisper of love,
    a whisper of joy.

Help me to be strong
    in the face of doubt
    in the dark of night.

Help me to be strong
    when others are weak.
Help me to show your love
    wherever I can. Amen.

Psalm 139:1-6
You have looked deep into my heart, Lord,
    and you know all about me.
You know when I am resting or when I am working,
    and from heaven you discover my thoughts.
You notice everything I do and everywhere I go.

Before I even speak a word,
* you know what I will say,*
* and with your powerful arm*
* you protect me from every side.*
I can't understand all this!
Such wonderful knowledge is far above me.

Lord, I hope you're there.
I'd feel really stupid if I was talking to myself!
It would be like being in a football ground
    when the team was playing away.
Or at a cinema when the film had finished two hours ago.
It might be like singing a song which had no tune,
    or trying to read a book in the dark.
All a bit pointless really!
So, God what is the point?
Why am I here?
Why do I feel so alone at times?
Why don't I hear you speak?
Why does everything feel such a mess?
Why?

I need to hear your voice.
I need to feel you near.
I need to know your love.
I need you.
But I don't know how any of that can happen.
I don't know what you want from me.
Still, here I am,
I'm listening – are you? Amen.

Lord, I know,
    no matter how I feel right now,
    whether it's a dustbin or a toilet,
    you see us for who we really are –
    precious people who you care for, every day.
It's difficult, I mean really difficult,
    to see above the mess and clutter
    that surrounds us.
I'm glad that you can see through the rubbish
    and look at my life with love.
Help me
    to trust,
    to see,
    to feel
    your love,
    no matter what I feel like. Amen.

Lord, I need a hug.
Sometimes I feel so lonely,
    and at times I feel it's me against the world.
I'm not sure I can carry that weight,
    I'm not the muscle-mad type!
Walking the extra mile and going the distance,
    is it really worth the effort?
You tell me it is,
    but you've been there before.
I don't like the sound of going through the pain barrier,
    is it worth getting to the other side?

So when you hug,
    don't hug too tightly, you might crumple my ego!
Only joking, or maybe I'm not.
If I make a move, will you move with me?
I'm not sure I can do this, I know that you can.
So, be with me each step of the way –
    hold me gently, don't let me go. Amen.

Love of God

This is something that is beyond understanding . . . well, it's totally beyond me anyway! After all, why should God who has so many other admirers, who possibly deserve a bit of TLC from him more than we do, care about us so much?

The only answer to that is to stop thinking like that and just accept the fact that God loves you no matter what! Just think of yourself as a piece of lost luggage that someone has taken the trouble to try and find; and when they eventually locate you amongst the other bits of emotional baggage they are so delighted to have found you that they go absolutely bananas. Sounds like party time to me.

Lord,
   you'll have to speak up,
   I can't hear you very well.
The sound of my own voice
   is almost deafening
   with a dustbin
   over my head.
It's not the best place to be,
   underneath a container for rubbish.
But perhaps it's the best place
   for the dustbin.
I wasn't pushed,
   I didn't stumble or trip.

I'm sitting here
  by choice
  because it's how I feel
  about myself.
Excuse me,
  what was that you said?
You want to come and join me?
Surely you can find a better place to be.
Pardon?
You can't think of anywhere better
  than here with me?
Hang on a minute, I'm coming out.
There's not enough room for two
  and anyway, I feel much better now there's you and me. Amen.

Father God,
  water is great
  when we're thirsty, we're hot, we're dirty,
  and when we're showing you
  that we don't want to hang on to anything
  which keeps us away from you.
Not our actions or our inactivity
  nor by giving in to thoughts that suggest
  we look away from you and your love for us.
We wash our hands
  as a symbol of our decision to follow you;
  as a symbol of love for your ways;
  as a symbol of thanks for your Son. Amen.

Psalm 13

How much longer, Lord, will you forget about me?
Will it be for ever? How long will you hide?
How long must I be confused and miserable all day?
How long will my enemies keep beating me down?
Please listen, Lord God, and answer my prayers.
Make my eyes sparkle again,
    or else I will fall into the sleep of death.
My enemies will say, 'Now we've won!'
They will be greatly pleased when I am defeated.
I trust your love, and I feel like celebrating
    because you rescued me.
You have been good to me, Lord
    and I will sing about you.

Lord,
    was that really necessary?
What on earth were you doing
    while I was trying to deal
    with a truck-load of garbage?
How could this have happened to me?
Why me? Isn't there someone else
    more deserving and better able
    to deal with this emotional sewer material?
I can't believe you let this happen.
One moment I was quietly minding my own business –
    well, that and the occasional verbal assessment
    of someone else's predicament –
    when, all of a sudden,

I'm up to my neck,
drowning, slipping, going under,
sliding and generally
having the sort of day
that I'm sure someone else
would appreciate more than me!
Hey! Don't interrupt.
I only paused for a breath.
Excuse me?
But, but . . .
oh, yeah, I do remember
how you helped me
the last time
to defy gravity, walk on water
and turn pigswill into a picnic.
Any chance of a repeat performance?
Sincerely yours . . . Amen.

Lord,
I'm watching,
observing,
looking at all these people
who don't seem to have very much in common.
But I'm still watching,
observing,
looking at such a variety of life passing by.
There are all sorts
of people
with their peculiar ways,

their idiosyncrasies,
their own way of doing things.
I really can't imagine
what you see in all of us.
We're such a ragbag of emotions,
of tastes, of styles.
(Not that many people have a sense of style!)
We're all so opinionated,
so devious,
so human.
But you love us just the way we are
and that knocks all my preconceived ideas about love
straight out of the window.
I don't know how you do it.
I think I know why you do it.
And I'm really glad you do
love me and him, and her and every single
twisted, hassled, frightened,
lonely, drained, wrecked, soiled, bedraggled, cracked,
phased, emotionally bankrupt
one of us.
I'm glad your heart is big enough
and your arms wide enough
to love and hold on to each one of us.
Thanks. Amen.

Prayer

Sometimes this subject is so smothered in ritual, tradition, theory and mystique that you wonder why God ever bothers with it. Is it really necessary to learn an ancient language or a dialect, which is rarely used outside of academic tea parties, simply to chat with our Creator about whatever is on our mind?

I remember reading somewhere that when God tore the veil in the Temple from top to bottom, he made a statement that it was his decision to have a relationship with us irrespective of who we were or where we came from. Surely the whole point of Jesus was to bring about a revolution in our relationship with God?

Take a look at the Psalms sometime. You'll find that David and the other psalmists got angry and annoyed at God, they ranted and raved, they told him just how they felt and, occasionally, also let him know that they thought he was totally awesome.

God doesn't sit in a building waiting for us to piously show our respect and say how sorry we are for being human. God is with us wherever we are and takes great delight in chatting with us. This relationship business is a twenty-four hour, two-way thing . . . don't ignore it.

Philippians 4:6-7
Don't worry about anything, but pray about everything. With a thankful heart offer up your prayers and requests to God. Then, because you belong to Christ Jesus, God will bless you with peace that no one can completely understand. And this peace will control the way you think and feel.

Lord,
   at times –
   well, if I'm honest, quite a lot of the time –
   I feel as if my head
   is in a blender.
My thoughts whizz around,
   until everything
   is in a complete mess.
It makes my stomach churn,
   and my legs feel odd.
If I could close my eyes,
   stick my fingers in my ears
   and scream,
   then I would, if it made
   any difference
   to the way I feel.
You may have noticed
   that when I tried that last time
   people gave me funny looks
   and wondered
   if I was quite right in the head.
I couldn't admit to them
   that my head felt full of spaghetti
   and if I had told them
   it wouldn't have made any difference.
But telling you how I feel
   seems to make all the difference.
Thank goodness for that. Amen.

Lord,
    when I'm honest –
    all right, I know that's not all of the time –
    but when I'm really honest,
    why do I feel that I'm always the loser
    when everyone else seems to benefit from the occasional
    'I'll borrow this for now and put it back sometime never!'
    I'm losing out, aren't I?
You know . . .
    from all of those little perks that make life
    sort of, well, worth the odd session of honesty?
    Who is going to know if I'm being honest anyway?
    I'm hardly likely to announce the fact that I was thinking,
    only thinking you understand,
    about helping myself to that box of chocolates;
    but I didn't.
    If I told everyone, then they'd think I wasn't to be trusted.
    Much easier to take the box and keep quiet,
    except for the internal combustion noises
    that a stomach on chocolate overload makes.
    You'd be the only person that knew
    and I could chat with you about it
    after the chocolate indulgence.
    But that's missing the point I suppose.
    Much better
    to have a chat with you
    before my stomach objects to my dishonest behaviour. Amen.

Relationships

Awkward. There's possibly quite a few other words you would use to describe the process whereby human beings subject themselves to regular scrutiny and frequently redefine vulnerability. When relationships work they're absolutely brilliant, the best thing since the invention of prunes and custard (relationships and prunes are a matter of taste and both can leave your stomach feeling decidedly dodgy). When they don't work (forget the prunes and co.) they can leave you feeling devastated, as if something has exploded inside of you (No! forget the prune bit). Whichever way you look at it, a relationship takes a lot of time, nurturing and plenty of loving care. It's worth it in the end, honest!

Lord, sorry!
I don't have to list all the things I'm sorry for,
    do I?
I'm just sorry, OK?
I'm not proud of my behaviour,
    or the way I speak, or don't speak!
It's not easy, you know,
    going out of my way to pass the time of day
    with people I'd rather not know;
    or stopping to help people who wouldn't stop for me.
How can I spend time with people
    who don't like the same things as me?
Who don't watch the same TV programmes?
Who don't dress as they should?
Who don't listen to the music that's good for their ears?

What's that you're saying?
Sorry, I can't quite hear you,
    I think I've got selective hearing.
Speak up, Lord,
    what's that . . . you love me?
Thanks, I really appreciate that.
Pardon? Could you repeat that?
Love who?
Oh! Sorry! Amen.

Lord,
    it's often difficult
    to know who's right and who's wrong.
Just as it takes two to argue,
    it takes two to agree
    to build the bridge
    which will join two islands
    that have been separated
    by an ocean of misunderstanding.
Please help us to learn
    how to build bridges,
    no matter how far
    or how wide
    the gap.
Help us to be willing
    to realise the loneliness
    of anger, of hurt and of damaged pride,
    so that we can be a continent of hope
    and not a cluster of islands in a raging sea. Amen.

Proverbs 13:20
Wise friends make you wise,
but you hurt yourself by going around with fools.

Lord,
here I am,
saying sorry, again,
for behaving like a cranky gorilla
at a toddlers' tea party.
I didn't mean to make anyone feel
as if they belonged
on another planet –
or even suggest that they should
see a vet.
You know how it is,
one thing leads to another
and before you know it,
bang! I've shot my mouth off,
again.
I wouldn't mind so much,
but I always feel so guilty
afterwards.
As if I've stolen something.
Maybe I have –
stolen something –
like another person's
happiness,
or their confidence.
As if I've screwed it up

and tossed it away like garbage.
I'm sorry, please help me.
Can we start again, like I know we should? Amen.

Lord, it's difficult enough
   trying to cope with myself
   without having to understand,
   appreciate, care and become friends
   with all those people who really
   get up my nose, irritate and generally
   make me feel as if I've eaten
   a few too many jam doughnuts.

Your idea of that funny word,
   you know, that *thingy* word,
   the one you talk about so much
   (I don't want to say the word,
   because if I do
   you just might make me behave
   like I know the word
   and want to act
   like that *thingy* word).

Why should I go out of my way
   to be *thingy*
   to everyone whom you *thingy*?
Thingy makes me feel funny
   as if I've done something
   odd, different, not normal,

something out of the ordinary
and definitely not the way to behave
if you want street-cred
with all those other people
who don't use that *thingy* word.

But just suppose,
    not for real you understand,
    just pretend that I knew what *thingy*
    really meant,
    I suppose it might, just might
    make a difference. Amen.

Proverbs 27:9
*The sweet smell of incense can make you feel good,
    but true friendship is better still.*

Father God,
    you know that at times I could scream,
    at other times I feel numb.
I'm not sure if some of my friends are enemies
    or if some of my enemies are friends!
It all gets a bit confusing.
You know that the best way to spread gossip
    is to tell your friend not to say a word!
Trouble is,
    if you don't share your thoughts with a friend,
    they get angry

and accuse you of not being open with them.
Don't get me wrong,
    I want friends around me,
    it's just that sometimes
    I'm not sure who I can trust.
There's only one thing for it . . .
If I tell you what's on my mind
    will you tell me what's on yours? Amen.

Lord,
    why is this relationship thingy
    so tough?
Come on, why couldn't you have sorted this out
    before you allowed two people
    to become mutually exclusive?
If you're honest,
    and isn't that something you're quite big on?
    you have to admit
    that we're an odd species.
I don't agree that women come from one planet
    and men from another.
I think they are from different universes.
Did you have a bit of a giggle
    when you took a rib from Adam
    and made him a companion?
I think you may have conned him
    by saying that it would only cost a rib,
    'cos you forgot to say
    it would cost him an arm and a leg later

just to keep her happy!
Hey, I'm only joking,
   it works both ways.
She likes to be flattered
   and given gifts
   while he's trying to find the courage
   to whisper, lovingly in her ear,
   he's supposed to be going down the pub with his mates.
Being honest
   is too tough at times.
To admit that you might,
   just a fraction, a teeny-weeny bit,
   be out of order,
   and saying it out loud,
   feels like you've just confessed
   to being a serial bone-cruncher
   (she's a vegetarian you know).
I know, I'm avoiding the issue,
   just like I do
   when me and my significant other
   have a blazing row
   about why it's OK
   for me to be wrong, and not admit it,
   when she is forced to plead guilty
   when she hasn't a clue
   what I'm on about.
Saying sorry
   through gritted teeth
   not only sounds strange
   but doesn't do your teeth any good either.

I need, no, I think we both need
  to ask for your help
  whenever we're finding the going tough,
  which is pretty much
  most of the time.
But all I can ask
  is that you'll be with us,
  love us, and hug us,
  when the last thing we feel like doing
  is hugging each other. Amen.

Trust

Trust, when left to experience, doesn't seem to prove a great deal.
There's no simple rule or technique that allows us to judge who we
can trust and who we can't. Usually, our experience tells us that we
can trust family and friends until, that is, one of them does something that crumbles our confidence in experience and shatters our
belief in trusting anyone.

What's the alternative? Do we trust no one, take nothing at face
value and suspect everyone of being devious, malicious and down-
right dishonest? Not a route to guarantee friends I think.

Trusting someone does mean making ourselves vulnerable, putting
our self-esteem at risk and allowing someone else to have access to
our life. Scary when you think about it!

God, it's not easy.
There seem so many things that get in the way.
It's difficult to understand,
    why you want to work with me.
I can't imagine what you have in mind
    when you say, 'Come with me'.
But you know me better than anyone,
    although there are some things I would rather you didn't know!
Even knowing all my doubts and fears,
    you still look my way.
I place all my obstacles and difficulties before you.
Deal with them.
Though they appear huge to me,

together we can work through them.
Thank you for trusting me.
Help me to trust you. Amen.

Lord,
    you know I get worried about things.
They might seem really daft to some people,
        but to me they are worse than
        a face full of spots.
I don't go out of my way to worry,
        it sort of stomps around my head,
        making itself known,
        just in case I try to ignore it.
Hiding my face in my hands doesn't seem to change things,
        I can't blink and make things go away.
I can't turn my back and hope they'll go away.
It never seems long
        before the finger of despair
        taps me on the shoulder
        and I'm faced with the reality
        of sinking under the ocean of my worry.

Help me, shield me,
        so that I can feel secure
        in your love.
I don't want to go it alone,
        or drown in anxiety.
I want to put my trust in you,
        I want to feel at peace
        with you. Amen.

Proverbs 3:5-6
*With all your heart and mind trust the Lord
    and not your own judgement.
Always let him lead you,
    and he will clear the road for you to follow.*

Lord,
    can I trust you?
You know, when things get hard,
    out of hand
    and just a bit messy?
Can I trust you
    when my head thumps
    from the millions of hassles
    that cloud my day?
Can I trust you
    when my eyes are tired and my brain aches
    and my feet want to give up and go home?
Can I trust you
    when I feel cold, lonely,
    unlovely, hurt and scared?
Can I trust you
    when everything I try to do
    and everything I try to say
    just make things worse?
Lord, can I trust you
    to keep me safe,
    to protect me from harm,
    to sort out the hassle and the grief?
Lord, be with me. Amen.

Lord,
   I often feel as if I'm standing
   in the middle of a football crowd.
The deafening roar
   hurts my ears
   and makes my head ache.
Sometimes it seems as if I'm in a dark tunnel
   without a light.
I can't see where I've been
   or where I should go.
I'm not too sure
   about putting my feet down
   when I can't see
   what I might be stepping in.
And then there are the really bad times
   when the football crowd
   have joined me in the tunnel
   and now I can't hear a thing
   or see anything,
   and no one can hear me shout.
But you, Lord,
   can perform miracles.
You can make yourself heard
   above the deafening noise,
   be seen in the darkest night,
   and can hear me when I whisper.
Be with me,
   teach me,
   listen to me
   as my heart beats to the rhythm
   of the Creator of the universe. Amen.

Psalm 37:3
Trust the Lord and live right!
The land will be yours and you will be safe.

Well, Lord, it's me again.
You know, the one who has a bag of chips on their shoulder.
I'm not depressed or anything,
    I'm used to looking and feeling
    like the contents of a dustbin.
It becomes a way of life,
    looking at everything through grime-coloured eyes.
I know I should be thankful for what I am,
    and what I've got, but I'm not.
Why does it seem as if I'm not quite,
    somehow, well sort of, you know,
    a full cream biscuit?
And, why does it seem like what I am
    isn't anywhere near as interesting,
    or amusing, or head-turning as anybody else?
Come to think of it,
    I don't stand out in a crowd,
    and I don't even stand out in a room on my own.
I feel as if people pay more attention to the wallpaper
    than they do to me.
But then this morning, I read that you are the one
    who put me together inside my mother's body . . .
    the wonderful way you created me.
Everything you do is marvellous . . .
Whoopee!

Mega whoopee!
A full cream biscuit whoopee!
Hang on a moment while I climb out of the dustbin.
Hello, it's me again.
I'm alive and I thought I really ought to say thanks.
Thanks for taking an interest in me,
   and loving me just the way I am. Amen.

Worship

If you were to ask twenty people what worship meant you'd get twenty different responses. There doesn't appear to be set formulas or prescribed actions that define worship for everyone. Sometimes, you can be with a group of people who express their faith in a way which feels appropriate to you. At other times, some people will behave in a way which seems wholly inappropriate to you. Some will say that you can only truly worship in a place that is set aside for such activity; others will claim that being surrounded by loads of people and swamped with images and objects make people feel insignificant and in no way inspire them to express their faith.

Worship would seem to be an expression of our hearts. That expression cannot be a constant emotion where we are forever declaring our happiness and thanks that God loves us. Surely we can express our hearts to God wherever we find ourselves? It's great to share our faith with other people and to express our hearts to God together. It's also great to be walking by a stream or along a mountain track and just get a sense of how awesome God really is. It's also neat to sit in a café, sipping a coffee, watching the world go by and realising that God has a fantastic sense of humour and just how much he loves every single person without question. Totally amazing!

Lord, thank you.
Although thank you doesn't really seem enough,
    considering that you didn't trust your lucky rabbit's paw,
    or keep your fingers crossed, just in case.

When you touched wood it wasn't for luck,
   or even to make sure that everything would work out all right.
You touched wood,
   the wood of the cross,
   to turn harm into good;
   to bring life where there was death;
   to give hope where there was doubt.
Lord, thank you. Amen.

Lord, it is easy to think that it gets dark too quickly,
   that clouds obscure the sun.
When it's night, someone somewhere else is enjoying the light.
Our darkness can often seem to last longer than everyone else's.
Help us to see.
Help us to open up the dark areas for your light to shine.
Help us to trust you when dark clouds gather on the horizon.
Be with us as the shadows give way
   to the brightness of your Son. Amen.

Psalm 63
You are my God. I worship you.
In my heart, I long for you,
   as I would long for a stream in a scorching desert.
I have seen your power and your glory
   in the place of worship.
Your love means more than life to me,
   and I praise you.
As long as I live, I will pray to you.

I will sing joyful praises and be filled with excitement
    like a guest at a banquet.
I think about you before I go to sleep,
    and my thoughts turn to you during the night.
You have helped me,
    and I sing happy songs in the shadow of your wings.
I stay close to you,
    and your powerful arm supports me.
All who want to kill me will end up in the ground.
Swords will run them through,
    and wild dogs will eat them.
Because of you, our God, the king will celebrate
    with your faithful followers,
    but liars will be silent.

Lord,
    sometimes trying to express my feelings
    makes me feel
    vulnerable,
    hurt,
    sensitive,
    stupid,
    useless.

But at other times I feel
    glad,
    happy,
    gobsmacked,
    astonished,

and, not very often,
    totally speechless.
Thanks for being there.
Thanks for being you.
Thanks for standing by me
    even when you have every right to walk away.
I may not always be honest with you,
    and I definitely can't be honest with some people.
But you know that grin I have
    hides a thousand hurts.

I like being real with you,
    because you are real to me
    even when I can't get a handle on you.
Thanks,
    thanks for being who you are.
Thanks from me, to you. Amen.

Lord,
    I can appreciate the colours
    in a field full of flowers.
I can smell the richness
    of the differing scents
    as the breeze blows across every plant.
I can hear an orchestra
    of sounds in the air,
    with each whisper of life
    giving an identity,
    a unique expression

of living
in a world of variety.
I appreciate the difference
in everything that surrounds me.
Each building, tree, flower or person
combines to make
a tapestry of existence.
Lord,
thank you for being
the Creator of all things,
the giver of life
and a Father to humanity
in a world of variety. Amen.

.